If I Had Only Known About Money Then

MITCHELL C HOCKENBURY

For Kickers: Learn from the mistakes of others

CONTENTS

INTRODUCTION

Thank you for reading this book. It isn't long, but it is powerful. My hope is you take the mistakes I have made in the past 25 years and apply the lessons learned to your own life. You will be far richer, and a better person, if you do.

Why the Book?

A few years ago, I was lamenting to myself how much of life I had wasted doing things wrong. I thought, "Man, if only I knew back when I was 20 what I know now, I would be so much farther ahead in the game of life." Well, no kidding! Doesn't everyone? But as I was stewing in my own misery, it hit me: I can't go back in time, but I can ensure the next 20 years aren't filled making mistakes that have already been made before.

I recognized I could think about what I wanted to be in life (in my case a financial planner and investment manager), and look up who is successful in that area. Would they be willing to sit down with me and tell me where they messed up and what they wished they knew 20 years ago? I set out to do just that, and a funny thing happened. Everyone I asked said yes. They were more than happy to share their experiences with me. I was thrilled and enthusiastic to put together their lessons learned so I would prosper going forward. To each of those people, and there are many, I am thankful. They have helped me as I continue on my path.

With that in mind, I decided to write this book. I want you to be successful with money. You will be able to apply the lessons I learned immediately. Best of all, this book isn't filled with long, drawn-out chapters. I didn't want to put together a boring book that wouldn't be read. I wanted something that could be read in one sitting and easily digestible. I wanted the concepts to be understood and *retained*. I wanted you, the reader, to avoid the mistakes that I made. It really doesn't matter if you are 22, 42, or 62 years old, if you heed the advice, you won't have to make the same mistakes I did, and you will be rewarded going forward.

Thank you, again, for reading. It is my aim that you get a great deal of value out of the small price you paid. I am certain of it. Last thing: read to the end where I have added a bonus section that is, perhaps, the most important concept for not only money, but life.

Warm regards,

Mitchell C Hockenbury

June 2017

1
DEBT IS WORSE THAN YOU THINK

You will, undoubtedly, read or hear experts tell you there are two kinds of debt: good debt and bad debt. I, too, have heard the following: a mortgage, student loans, and auto loans (if needed for work) are good debt. Credit cards and unsecured debt are bad. "Stay away from bad debt and only take on good debt," *they* say. This is a bad way to think. A better way to think: Stay away from debt like it's the plague! Get the following message into your head: Debt is bad, debt is bad, and debt is bad. This should be your mantra. Once you get it clearly into your head, you can make an exception for it a handful of times in your life. Read that last line again. You get five exceptions over the course of your life. If you only have a punch card with 5 holes to punch each time you take on debt, you are forced to be selective.

You can take on debt in the form of a mortgage, but it comes with a big *BUT*. **BUT**, you need to think about the mortgage in terms of a down payment, a fixed rate, and preferably a 15-year loan. A home you call your own can be a wonderful thing. It can also be an anchor to your life goals. Don't let a home weigh you down at the expense of savings goals and fun! My wife and I once lived in one of the most beautiful places in the United States: Monterey, California. Not only did we live in this amazing place; we lived in an idyllic setting: on top of a mountain with views of the Pacific Ocean. It was spectacular, but we were house poor. We couldn't travel, we couldn't go out to eat often, and we couldn't go out to have drinks with friends. We had people come over and they enjoyed the views, but when you live there every day, it is nice to get out sometimes!

You will read, or be told, you can afford this much house (insert dollar amount here). That doesn't mean you should spend that amount on a house. You need to determine the amount you can afford in a monthly payment. Additionally, you need to think about how much utilities cost. (Hint: call the local utility company and give them the address of the home you intend to purchase. Ask the <u>level payment cost</u>: this is the total cost in a year divided by 12. Now you have the monthly rate for budgeting!) How much are the property taxes? (Hint: call the county assessor's office, or go online, and give them the address. They will tell you the yearly property tax. Divide by

12. Now you have the monthly rate for budgeting!) How much will insurance cost? (Don't go with a general idea based on what Zillow provides; instead, call your insurance provider and ask. Hint: ask how much your automobile insurance will cost. It most likely will change. The last house I purchased provided me with a multi-policy discount, but it was nullified by the higher auto cost.) But wait, there's more! Is there an HOA (homeowner's association dues), will you do yard work or will you hire that out? HOA is easy to add to the budget; the yard work requires you to obtain at least three bids (trust me, always get 3 bids!). Finally, you need to set up an emergency fund for the house. Think, at a minimum, the deductible for homeowner's insurance, and better, the cost of replacing the roof or air conditioner. You should have that amount of money set to the side, and preferably, 20% of the purchase price of the home to avoid paying PMI (Private mortgage insurance). Add it all up and determine if it makes sense to buy a home. Don't do it just because it is "good debt."

Student Loans

Are student loans good debt? You need to think of it as a return on investment (ROI). I love education. I have two undergraduate degrees, a master's degree (MBA) and I have several professional certifications. My grand total in student loan debt over the entire course of my life: $12,000. I took on $12k and find myself making a six digit per year income. I recognize I would not make that much money without the education. Conversely, my wife went to a private university that charged $17,000 per year to graduate with a degree that would get her a job making $25,000 per year. In that case, she would have a $68,000 student loan making $21,000 per year after tax. This is not a good ROI. She could have simply gone to work at a department store and made the same amount of money and she wouldn't have the $68,000 loan. Not all student loans are "good debt." If you will make more money in salary (a great deal more) after obtaining your degree, then perhaps it was good to take on the loan. Otherwise, it is not.

The Real Reason Debt Is Bad

Now let me tell you the REAL reason "good debt, bad debt" is a poor way of thinking: it leaves open the idea there is good debt. This can lead you to rationalize credit card debt. "I don't have the money for this dress, but I _need_ it for the job interview." Next thing you know, you have credit card debt. Please take my word for it: this is a slippery slope that leads to bad places. You can rationalize the irrational once you start. I can give you hundreds of examples from my own life, but I won't. I don't need to because you know it is true. Deep down you know. For those who don't have, and have never had, credit card debt, ask a friend and you'll see. Don't believe me? Ask *anyone* who has credit card debt how it happened. They won't know! They will begin with *sort of* an idea, but if you ask them to itemize it, just in a "ballpark" way, they will not have an answer.

We live in a consumer-driven economy. You are inundated with commercials. There are companies employing Harvard MBA types (a whole bunch of them) that sit around a conference room table for 12 hours a day trying to figure out how to separate you from your dollar. They are paid a lot of money. You are no match for them if you are not aware. You really are no match if you don't subscribe to the "no debt is good debt" mantra I wish upon you.

You can make a handful (think 5) of exceptions over your lifetime. For instance, a nice 15-year fixed-rate mortgage that is less than 30% of your paycheck. That's one! You don't have many more chances remaining.

If I had only known…

…about debt being bad, I wouldn't have taken on car loans or gone into credit card debt tens of thousands of dollars…or…

2
SAVINGS RATE IS THE MOST IMPORTANT METRIC

This is going to be the most important thing I write, so I hope my powers of persuasion can reach you, because if you can grasp this, you will be ahead of nearly anyone (actually everyone) you meet. This is earth-shattering stuff. When you learn to think with this on the forefront of your mind, you are powerful. By the way, if you don't fully grasp this when I am done, reach out to me. I can explain it differently or point you in the right direction to others who will explain it in another manner. It IS that IMPORTANT regardless of your income level.

Traditional Approach

Most advisors will tell you to save 10-15% of your income. That is sound advice. Today, the average person saves 5.7% of their after-tax income[1] (U.S. Bureau of Economic Analysis). If we flip that to the pre-tax rate, it is just under 7%. Let's use rounded numbers: people save 7% and experts advise 10-15%. I say that is not enough. Let me walk you through the math of the typical advice.

Pretend you just graduated from college. You are 22 and get a $50,000/year job. Great on you. You are following traditional advice and saving 10% of your income ($5,000) and earn 10% each year on your investments for the next 43 years. You are now 65 (typical retirement age) and find you have nearly $3,000,000 in your 401(k). Nice work! Notice you didn't get any raises and we aren't looking at inflation (assume they cancel each other out). You probably took out a 30-year mortgage and hopefully have it paid off by now. You did well. You can retire.

The 10% rule worked for you in our math example, but life is a bit different than that, right? Some won't start working until later in life, some will not save 10% each year, and some will have copious amounts of debt along the way, while some won't begin their first job making $50,000. None of that matters. It is personal finance, and it is *personal* to you. The takeaway is that you worked 43 years.

---

[1] https://www.bea.gov/newsreleases/national/pi/2017/pi0117.htm

I want you to think in a different way. I want you to retire early, or at least have the opportunity to do whatever fulfills you. You can gain financial independence (FI). FI is the point where you can continue working if you want, or you can sit around all day, or something in between. Here is how you do it: save 40%, 50%, 60% or more! NO, I'm not kidding, not even a little bit. Imagine if you saved 50% of your income. You would have a pile of money and in short order. Best of all, it really isn't that hard. Stay with me and push the "I believe" button for another five minutes. If you don't believe me at the end, then so be it. You can join the other 99% out there following the traditional advice and falling short. But, if you want to really be special and differentiate yourself, read on!

Here are some easy ways to save 50%. If you marry another working person, why not save the other's paycheck? Each of you made it on one salary before you got married, and two people aren't that much more expensive. Think about this: it is only incrementally more for food (not twice as much; you get to share the bottle of ketchup instead of both of you buying one individually, right?), incrementally more for utilities (water usage is a bit more, electricity barely more), but housing is the same (two live in the same house as one), and internet and cable is the same, so it isn't that hard to combine expenses. Or, think of it another way: you have been living cheaply as a college student, so continue to live that way for a few more years. Don't rush out and buy stuff that isn't needed. Take a minimalist approach (see Chapter 4: Less Stuff = More Money).

High income producers: You have a gift of making a lot of money. Congratulations. Seriously, well done. Now, you can go and spend and spend, or you can take a few years to build up a sizable nest egg and then go spend money. Let's say you make $150,000 (more is better, but you'll get the idea at this income level). Instead of moving into a neighborhood where everyone with your income can afford upper-middle class homes, what if you remain in a nice, clean, and safe apartment for 5 years? Or, buy a modest townhouse or condo. Sure you qualify for a $500,000 house, but what if you bought a $175,000 home? You could live off $75,000 and pay down the mortgage with the other half. In three years, you own the home outright. Two years later, you have over $120,000 in the bank. Five years later, you have more than half a million dollars. Why not build up a million-dollar portfolio with zero debt, then go out and buy a $500,000 house, a new car, furnish it and rent out the townhouse? You'd be in your mid 30s and rolling in the dough. Now drop your savings rate from 50% to 20% if you are so inclined. You just gave yourself a huge raise (60%!). How much easier would life be?

You must begin to think in terms of financial independence. Forget worrying how much you earn on your investments. Chasing high returns on investments is a great way to underperform (see Chapter 12: Indexing Is Best). When you think "savings rate" and how you can increase it, you are doing your future self a huge favor.

As a side benefit, if you spend less, you will focus on the necessities and steer clear of silly purchases you will only use a few times and throw away or accumulate. There will be less stuff to get in your way. You should be purposeful and intentional in your spending. Consequentially, this is a byproduct of happiness.

Running the Numbers

Preaching aside, let's do the numbers in a different way with no investing—just stuffing it under the mattress. If you are saving the traditional 10% every 10 years, you have saved 1 year of income. Think about it: 10 x 10 = 100. In ten years, you have saved enough to take a year off. But what about saving 50%? Now, every two years you have bought a year off! It gets really exciting when you add compound interest (see Chapter 10: Compounding Early Is Vital).

Now let's add some compounding and figure out the *real* numbers. If you earned an investment return of 10% and saved 50% of your income, in 12 years, you will have roughly $534,600. Do you realize what that half million dollars will get you? Financial independence! You will have enough to replace your spending. Read that again. You will have $535,000 and you won't have to work again! That is financial independence! You can do what you want to do. No boss, no *I have to*, nothing. Don't believe me? Let's do the math. You make $50,000 and save 50%. That means $25,000 goes to savings and you spend the other $25,000 to live. Twelve years later, you have $534,600. Remember, you need $25,000 to live (actually less as you are taxed, but whatever). If you take 4.7% out each year, you will have $25,126 to spend. Congrats, you just got a $126 raise. More importantly, you can chase your passions and do the things that really mean something to you. You no longer have to work for "the man."

Another way of thinking about this is in multiples of your spending. You were spending $25,000 each year. If you multiply it by 22, you get $550,000. Therefore, whatever you are spending each year multiplied by 22 equals the amount you need to be financially independent. So, if you are spending $80,000 each year, you are going to need $1,760,000.

If you aren't making the connection, let me help make it clear: If you spend less money each year, you will need less money saved. You should incentivize yourself to spend less money, and save more, each year. Better yet, make the challenge each month. Little changes will make a big difference later in life. This chapter is vitally important to your financial future, regardless of your age or income level. If you have failed to fully grasp what I am writing, please reach out to me. I can provide you with resources to hear it another way.

If I had only known…

…about the importance of savings rates, I would have retired 8 years ago.

3

BUDGET = GUILT-FREE SPENDING

If you are like me, you already know you need a budget to obtain all the benefits budgeting entails. Additionally, if you are like me, you get a little depressed when looking at ALL the line items listed on sample budgets. It all seems so constrictive! There are books written on budgeting with hundreds of pages, making it feel quite overwhelming. So, I never budgeted. Instead, I would wing it. Seriously. I had an inkling of an idea of how much I was spending in certain categories, but didn't know exact totals. Additionally, I didn't know if I was overspending, because I was "ball-parking" it. But nothing convinced me I had to budget until I began to do it.

Being Proactive

Now I understand what the fuss is all about. If you know exactly where all your money is going each month, you can manage it. No longer am I reactive. Instead, I am proactive because of budgeting. I don't wonder if I am overspending or whether I am saving enough. I know because I have allocated the money ahead of time. There are a couple of ways to budget, but I am all-in with zero-based budgeting. It is quite simple: you write down how much you will earn in the next month (super easy if you are salaried and know exact amounts in each paycheck, but still works if you are hourly. It only is different for irregular income workers such as those who are commission-based). Next, you spend every dollar. You spend it ahead of time in excel or on paper. You know how much your mortgage or cable bill will be each month, but there are some things that aren't obvious like utility bills. However, with thought, you can figure out the average utility bill. Subtract each line item from the total income amount brought in and you have zero dollars at the end. If there is money left over, allocate it to savings or debt repayment. I have it down to all the yearly memberships, too. For instance, I have Amazon Prime and Costco memberships. I literally save $8.25 each month in preparation for the $99 Amazon yearly membership.

Guilt-free Spending

Now that you have spent the money before it comes in, when it comes time to pay a bill or spend money on entertainment (going to the movies for instance), you don't have any guilt. You already agreed with your significant other you would spend that amount. You don't have to worry they are looking at you sideways when you walk in with a shopping bag. When my wife and I weren't budgeting, we were having trouble making ends meet. If she walked in the house with a Williams-Sonoma bag, I would feel my blood pressure rise. Now we have money that each of us can spend on whatever we wish without consulting the other person. As long as you don't violate the trust by overspending that amount, it doesn't matter what is bought. Today when she walks in with one of those bags, I simply assume it is her amount to blow on whatever she wishes. As a matter of fact, because you have already "spent" the money beforehand, *she has to spend the money*! Think about it: there is zero guilt when you have to do something, right?

Additional Benefits

Aside from the guilt-free spending, there are other benefits to budgeting. You have logically thought out where you are allocating your money. You are not influenced by marketers trying to separate you from every one of your dollars. The emotions remain in check. You have agreed to the spending sums with your significant other, or with yourself. This means you are in it together as a team. By working on the budget together, you get buy-in and grow together as a couple. Plus, by doing it as a team, the other person is less likely to derail the budgeting process by overspending. This becomes a contract between the two of you. Lastly, it provides introspection. I can look at the budget and ask myself if the spending that is occurring is worth it. Is it good to spend $200 each month on alcohol? "Probably not," I told myself and not only has my savings increased, my waistline has decreased. That's a win-win!

You don't need a hundred pages to tell you why to budget, or even how to budget. This chapter sums it up by simply explaining the best reason to budget, and that is spending without guilt. People think it is too hard or restrictive. I can attest it is not hard and it is not restrictive; rather, it is freeing. Contact me if you need help setting up a budget. It is not difficult, and a couple of fantastic resources include Dave Ramsey, You Need a Budget, Mint.

If I had only known...

...about budgeting, I would have saved myself feelings of worry, guilt, and anxiety. Plus, I would have significantly more money today!

4
LESS STUFF = MORE MONEY

There is a tendency for each of us to hold onto as much as possible, with one exception: money. Why is that? Well, we live in a consumer-driven environment with sayings such as, "he who dies with the most toys, wins." It is pretty easy to see this is not going to be helpful to your savings and investing accounts. We are inundated with ads telling us if we just had this gizmo, it would make us happier. Intuitively, we know this is not the case, but we still go about accumulating things. We buy the newest iPhone when the iPhone we currently have works just fine. But, it doesn't do (fill in the blank) and it isn't as sexy looking. So, we go out and buy it, but it doesn't end with the latest gadget. Our homes are filled with things we don't need. Open your closet, or worse, your storage room, and tell me there aren't dozens of things you never use but think you may in the future. Further, tell me there aren't things in there that you *had* to have when you bought it, but as you look at it now, you don't know *why*.

I am not here to deny you the latest iPhone, if that is what you wish. I simply want to get you to think a bit differently. Going forward, I want you to buy less *stuff* and instead, buy things you will *actually* use. Don't buy on a whim. Be deliberate in your purchases. Think them over before you commit to the buy. Do you already have something that works? If so, don't replace it until it breaks.

What I have found is if you cull the stuff you have, get rid of things you haven't used in the last six months, you will find that having less things will give you a sense of peace. You will find that the organized shelves in your storage closet of things you do use from time-to-time (like camping gear or Christmas decorations) and not things you never use or regret buying (thigh-master anyone?) will give you emotional comfort. Conversely, looking at a bunch of stuff you don't use will create anxiety and guilt.

Going forward, you will find simplicity is the key. Buy things that have multiple purposes. Many years ago, my wife just *had* to have an asparagus steamer. I didn't even know there was such a thing. Further, we never ate asparagus. Somehow, she got it in her head that if we had an asparagus steamer, we would eat more of it and we would benefit because asparagus is good for you. Well, she bought one from Williams-Sonoma (or as I call it, the Hundred-Dollar Store because you can't leave there without spending a hundred dollars) and we used it a grand total of 1 time as it didn't have any other uses. We lugged that thing around from move-to-move and finally, I said, "Can we get rid of this?" She complied and we haven't had a need for it since. Two things happened: first, she was happier because she no longer felt the guilt over buying it each time she saw it, and second, we now eat asparagus 3-4 times each month. We cook it on the grill and it tastes good! It tastes better than when cooked in the steamer.

The Real Benefit

I haven't even touched on the biggest benefit to having less stuff: more money! Of course you will have more money if you are purchasing less stuff, right? I am not telling you to buy the cheapest stuff that will break down causing you to buy it all over again. Additionally, I am not telling you to purchase the "best of the best" of whatever particular product. If you did, you may not have more money. Find the happy medium. Buy the best for the money and no more. Find products that will fill more than one need if possible. Buy only when it is a *need* and not a *want*. *(Make sure you understand the difference between the two.)* Finally, just because you have a 2000-square-foot home doesn't mean you have to fill every square foot! Be deliberate in your purchases, get rid of things that you don't need, and don't buy on a whim.

If I had only known…

…about stuff, I wouldn't buy things without putting thought behind the purchase to determine if it is truly needed. I would have less stuff, but the stuff I have would be used, which would provide the benefit of liking what I have and not having guilt because I blew the money. Yeah, I'm talking about you asparagus steamer.

5

A CAR DOES NOT DEFINE YOU

I like cars. I like fast cars, luxurious cars, tough-looking trucks, and electric vehicles. I guess you can say I have bought into the marketing out of Detroit, Michigan. It took me way too long to realize, though, that a car cannot make me happier...it cannot define me. A vehicle gets you from one place to the next. That is it.

Master Marketers

Car companies have mastered the art of marketing that we should drive around in $40,000 machines that sit around for 22 or more hours a day. For some reason, we believe the hype we will be cooler, sexier, more liked, more *whatever*, if we buy a new car. The car companies have taken a base car and convinced us to upgrade to one of the other four "models" of the same car. Have you ever looked at the fine print in a car commercial? The commercial boldly splashes "starting at $23,500" across the screen, but at the bottom in 5-point font it says, "Priced as shown: $47,876." Holy smokes that's a big difference. Like a whole other car difference.

It's the Same Car!

It finally dawned on me when I "upgraded" my wife's 1995 Toyota Camry to a 2002 Lexus ES300. For her, it was her dream car. She loved everything about the darn thing. So, we saved up to buy it with cash. It was sweet looking, no lie, but I immediately noticed a number of oddly similar things: the steering wheel looked just like the Camry (except it had an "L"), the turn signals, the knobs, the seats…lo and behold, it was the same car! It really was. Basically, we upgraded to a more expensive Camry. Worse, if a part was needed, I'd call the Lexus dealership and be quoted one price, then call Toyota and get a price nearly half as much. You could have the same part for much less in a Toyota box than in the Lexus box. I was a chump.

New Thinking

Now, we buy used vehicles that are dependable and steer clear of luxury cars. I marvel when I sit at a stoplight in my 14-year-old car and see someone with in-transit tags and recognize they most likely spent $33,560 (average new car price in 2017, according to Kelley Blue Book), with a loan (ugh, interest!), with high costs to maintain and repair, and they will pay for it over 5 years at which point, they will trade it in and restart the process.

Why put so much money into a car when the impression is so fleeting? You are reading this book so you can see through the matrix car companies push. When a friend or coworker gets a new car, I usually say, "Nice car, looks cool," but inside I am always wondering why they bought it. Why harm yourself by paying so much for a thing that drops in value and simply gets you from one place to the next? I know the answer, because I used to fall victim to it myself. No more.

If I had only known...

...about cars, I wouldn't have paid $12,500 for a brand new 1994 Nissan Sentra or $13,500 for a 1993 Jeep Grand Cherokee Limited, or $32,000 for a new Ford F-150 Lariat. That's over $58,000 for cars collectively worth $8,000, and that's without factoring interest payments and lost savings!

6
SAYING NO TO FRIENDS IS VIRTUOUS

My wife and I are asked all the time to go out to eat or get drinks with friends. We have a small child who needs a babysitter, so these things have to be planned. Additionally, there are costs associated with dinner, coffee, movies, etc. Aside from the event itself, a babysitter's costs can add up. We budget for entertainment each month, but that money can go rapidly, and if there is something that "just came up," we may not have the cash. This puts us in a predicament. We can borrow from another spending category, or say no.

Saying No

If we choose to borrow from another spending category, inevitably we are left without enough cash for that item. We chose to spend the money on that category during our budget meeting, after all. But, isn't saying no a detriment to the friendship? Does it make us look as though we don't have any money? Will we be left out of future invitations? These are the questions my wife and I had. Though we don't know if we have been left out of future invitations (only the friends would know), we haven't seen any degradation of our friendships. In fact, the opposite usually occurs.

Ramifications of Saying No

If we simply explain we did not budget for (whatever the invitation) and do not have the money, we have found a couple of things happen. First, we find people are ok with us saying no. Second, they may adjust the invitation doing something free because they simply wanted to hang out with us. Other times, we find people are intrigued by our discipline and more so, we find them interested in talking about budgeting. We will get the reply, "Boy, we sure need to start doing that, too." This opens a whole new conversation. This conversation leads to us telling our story of being undisciplined and overspending years ago until we determined we didn't want to live in debt any longer. We explain how we haven't had a credit card balance in a decade. This is how we are able to go on fancy European vacations and live in a nice home.

By simply being open and honest about our finances, we are able to encourage others to do the same with theirs. This has led to a virtuous cycle for us in that we say no to the unexpected spending which causes our friends to do something free, which holds them accountable for their spending, which leads to proper planning the next time out. Additionally, it encourages our friends to save and get out of debt and to learn that "keeping up with the Joneses" is a non-starter for us. Because they are friends with us, they realize they don't have to impress us with new things or spending. In fact, they quickly realize we are most impressed when they tell us how much they save! We get excited for them to get out of debt and cheer them on. This adds depth to our relationship as they learn what excites us, and we can help each other through struggles rather than the potentially shallow relationship that can occur when spending without thought takes place. Caveat: We enjoy going out with people. There are few things more enjoyable than a nice night out with friends. The point is there are limits to this for us as money is finite. If we have the cash in our entertainment fund, we say yes. It is simply we have found it is ok to say no. It is something we had to learn because in the past, we would always say yes, even to the detriment of our budget and savings plan. We learned to simply be honest and explain the situation. It is ok to say no. Plus, we aren't social outcasts.

If I had only known...

...about saying no, I would have deepened my relationships, stayed out of the race to keep up with the Jones,' and encouraged others to budget at a much younger age. The side benefit: I'd have more money today to take those same friends out to dinner and pick up the tab.

7

COMPOUNDING EARLY IS VITAL

At the early age of 22, I had a firm grasp of the power of compounding. I understood that time is the most valuable asset when it comes to building great amounts of wealth. I read examples laying out the argument quite simply:

Two 22-year-olds: Savannah vs Curtis. Savannah diligently began saving at 22 (because she read this book) and put away $5000 per year into a Roth IRA. When she turned 32, she stopped saving money. She had a brain fart and forgot all she had learned reading this book a decade ago. But, she let it grow on its own earning 10% the entire time until she retired at age 65 (from age 22 to 65). Curtis did not have this book, nor the guidance from a reader, and waited until 32 to save and invest. He put away $5000 per year and earned the same 10% return. The only difference (besides starting later), is Curtis continued to save *every* year until age 65. He saved for 33 years! In total, Savannah saved $50,000 (10 years x $5000) and Curtis saved

$165,000 (33 years x $5000) Curtis must have come out ahead, right? Nope, when they both turned 65, Curtis has $1,111,257 versus Savannah's $1,850,645.

Let's look at that closely, because it is really important that you understand what is happening here: Curtis saves $165K vs Savannah's $50K, but she ends up with $740K more! What the heck just happened here? This is compounding. By having an extra decade to compound onto itself, Savannah's $50k is worth $79,687 by the time Curtis invests his first dollar. By the end of Curtis's first decade (Savannah's second), he will have the same as she did when he began saving, but even though she stopped saving, her investments *compounded* at 10%. His $79,687 compares to her $206,687. Even though he continues to save money, he cannot overcome the gap. Time is on Savannah's side.

This Is Vitally Important

I know this topic quite well as I studied it in college graduating with a finance degree. What I didn't understand before, and wish someone would have clubbed me over the head with, is it is <u>vital</u> to begin early. It is crucial. IT IS CRITICAL! I cannot emphasize this enough. It is terribly important.

If you are reading this book, don't just be "smarter" because you know; put it into practice, today! That is where I went wrong. Like so many young people, I didn't understand time. I thought I would always be young. Not in the strange world of immortality, but I *felt* younger than I was. Additionally, I thought I could out-save and out-earn my way to more money. I was wrong. I didn't diligently begin investing until Curtis's age. I cannot go back in time, and neither can you, but you can begin today.

Change Yourself, Change Your Family

I really don't care if you are 22 or 52 years old. You need to begin saving money. You cannot change time. There are certain variables to compounding: interest, dollar amount saved, starting amount, additional savings, and time. You can adjust any except time—the clock keeps ticking. So, what will you do about it? I say, do something! Begin now. Don't sit around any longer.

Personally, I am doing something radically different to ensure my daughter will learn my lesson. I am opening a Roth IRA for her even though she is a minor. As long as she has earned income, she can contribute to the Roth. Imagine your son, daughter, grandchild, or niece/nephew—what if they put the money they earned over the summer into a Roth IRA? What kind of benefit could that provide? What will that have taught them compounding-wise? Let's run the numbers and you determine if it is worth it.

Your aspiring entrepreneur child babysits or mows lawns for 3 months this summer, earning a cool thousand dollars. Next, let's pretend they began this enterprise at the age of 12 and repeated when they are 13, 14, and 15. At age 16, they get a "real" job at McDonald's making $8 per hour. They work 30 hours a week (should be more, but they are kids, right?) and save $2,000 over the summer after spending some of their hard-earned cash. Now they are off to college for 4 years and don't save anything. When they graduate 4 years later, they get the first "real, real" job and make $40,000. They learned from Chapter 2, Savings Rate Is the Most Important Metric, to save 50% or more, but I am playing a very conservative game here to show you that this stuff is easy if you have someone guide you (or you put this book in their hands at a young age). Last assumption: they earn 10% each year. Here are the results:

12-15 years old, saved $4000 ($1k each summer, 4 summers) worth $4,641.

16-18 years, saved $6,000 ($2k each summer, 3 summers) plus the initial $4,641 = $12,797.

Stop and think for a moment. Your kid has saved $10,000 and it is worth $12,797. That $2,797 in earnings is more than a summer's worth of savings. Do you think they might begin to understand making money work *for* them? I am sure of it. That is a big deal.

Back to the example: They go to college, make good grades and graduate 4 years later. They were lazy in their off-time and didn't work so they didn't add anything, but the account now has $18,736! That is real money. It grew by the amount they were contributing each summer! Think about that again: The value grew by $6000 without adding a dime. That is the same amount saved during four years of high school! Think it might be easy to convince them to save 15% of their pay upon graduating college? Might they be open to what was learned in chapter three? You bet. But let's play the game until they are age 32.

No raises are given. They earn $40,000 per year and put away $5,500 each year to the Roth IRA (that is the contribution limit which is less than 15% of their pay). At age 32, they will have $144,222. Of that amount, they only saved $70,000. So more than half of the money is *earnings*! Do you see the impact that can play out over their 30s? This is powerful stuff, but if it isn't learned early, it moves into the regret phase. By the way, if this kid simply continues to save $5,500 each year, at age 65, the account will have $4,571,961.

If I had only known…

…about the power of compounding, I would have started in my twenties and never halted. I would have hundreds of thousands of dollars more today and would have shared this knowledge with people sooner.

8

YOU DON'T HAVE TO GO ALONE

When I first began investing, I thought only rich people could afford to have an advisor. My first foray into the markets occurred while I worked at an online brokerage firm during the run-up to the Internet Bubble. The company was a do-it-yourself brokerage; they couldn't dispense advice, so I began to study investing on my own. I learned a great deal from it, but in hindsight, I wished I hadn't.

Tough Lessons

Since I didn't have the half a million or so dollars I thought was needed to afford an advisor, I began with following the advice of magazines. This led me to my first lesson: don't buy last year's winner. I saw the cover of *Money* magazine with the best-performing mutual fund from the previous year on the cover. It had gone up 500%! That sounded good to me, so I bought. One year later, my investment lost 90%.

I later bought several individual stocks after reading investment reports from analysts covering the companies. My next lesson was learned: stock analysts give buy recommendations and very few sell recommendations. This is because of the money made on the sell-side of their firms. It is not in the analyst's interest, financially, to give poor investment grades on the companies. Lesson two: Don't go off an analyst's recommendation.

Later, the company I worked for purchased a technical analysis company that helped track every up and down tick stocks made throughout the day. Based off the trends, it predicted the future short-term movements. This is trend, or technical, analysis. Third lesson: don't day trade. Moving in and out of the market is akin to gambling.

A Helpful Hand

If I had simply found an advisor that charged me 1% each year to place me into low cost index funds allocated in a diversified manner and keep me there through the ups and downs of the market, I would have come out way ahead (see Chapter 12: Indexing Is Best). I thought I would be a chump to pay someone to basically do nothing. I mean, once you are in the investments, aside from rebalancing each year, what would that person do for me? A lot, actually. Simply having a person to rationally speak with when I wanted to do something risky would be worth the money. Additionally, when the markets went down and I wanted to sell, having that person available to talk me out of it, and instead, add more money, would be well worth the cost.

What Would I Pay?

As I type this today, I am 42 years old. I am wondering how much I would pay today so my 22-year-old self would have done the right thing and sought sound advice? Without question, I would pay $100,000. I'd pay it right now and it would be a steal. My 22-year-old self wouldn't have had to pay that amount; instead, he could pay a conservative financial advisor to help guide him to sacrifice a little and properly invest. And 20 years later (today), I would have far more money than I presently do. In fact, my alternate reality 42-year-old self would be giggling right now at the small amount of money ($100k) paid.

If I had only known…

…about investing on my own, I would run to the nearest fee-only financial advisor willing to take me on as a client. I would follow that person's advice and be much wealthier today.

9

CONDUCT AN ANNUAL REVIEW

New Year's resolutions are for chumps! As I write this sentence the month of April has begun. I wonder how many people's resolutions are still in place, or have they gone the way of resolutions past? I'd bet for the majority out there (you included), your resolutions are old news. Why beat yourself up thinking about how you failed again? I understand that thinking because I used to have it. That is until I began to conduct an annual review. I have to credit Chris Guillebeau, creator of *The Art of Non-Conformity*, as he wrote a blog post[2] a number of years ago instructing people how to conduct an annual review (it is still a top article; google it!). When I read it, a light clicked on in my head. Bingo! Why wasn't I doing this before? I've now done it four times and I can tell you my life is much more productive, with the first quarter of this year (2017) being the most productive of any. The funny thing is that I am busier than ever.

---

[2] https://chrisguillebeau.com/how-to-conduct-your-own-annual-review/

A Better Way to Reach Goals

Pretend you have been hired by You, Inc. to conduct an annual review of your performance for the company. That is what it looks like. In December of each year, I hole up in a hotel room (I have a wife and a small child who will distract me at home) and conduct an introspective look at the year. What have I accomplished this year and what did I set out to do but didn't? Why was the accomplishment successful? Why were things I did not complete left undone? I perform a bit of post-mortem analysis. How far did I get when I stopped working on it? Was there a change of heart? Was I lazy?

By looking over the course of the year, I am able to firmly figure out where I stand. I break things out into the following categories: money, spousal relationship, parental relationship, friends and family, career, health, and retirement.

Next, I think about where I am heading and what I want to be "when I grow up." I think 10 years out. What does it look like? What makes me happy? How am I fulfilled? What am I doing for work? Here, I seem to be relationship-oriented. That is good! It means those things are important and need to be worked and developed the same as your weight and finances. Then I turn the attention to 5 years out. If I am going to be "x" in 10 years, where am I in 5, I ask. Five year out goals will certainly be more tangible. Finally, I think in terms of what will need to happen in the next year for me to meet those 5- and 10-year goals? This is backwards planning and allows me to understand, fully, what will need to be accomplished to meet my goals.

With the goals in mind, I narrow every category to 3-5 sub-goals and then break them down to baby steps to get there. For instance, I am writing a book. I want the manuscript ready for the back and forth editing process of finalizing by July 1st. Therefore, I need to break it down by chapter, and that allows me to plan for spending one week to write 25 pages. That would be 5 pages per work day. Now I have something tangible on which to base my annual review. Did I do it, or not?

Monitoring Progress

Next comes the monitoring process. At the end of the month (give or take a few days, I'm not that strict), I can assess myself. Am I on track or off the rails? Do I need to adjust the plan or not? This keeps me from allowing too much time between fails. If I give myself some grace to slack, then I am more likely to begin again. I simply tell myself to start new today. I treat myself as I would a subordinate. Then I encourage myself to go. I don't beat myself up. Consequently, it is easier to maintain momentum when I am tracking progress. Lastly, I will do a quarterly review to see where I am. This will allow the annual review to be more accurate, enabling me to fine-tune the next year's goal setting. It is a virtuous cycle.

If I had only known…

…about goal setting, I would have conducted an annual review boosting my productivity and wasting less of my time.

10
FORGET LOVE

I wish I would have forgotten love for one day before getting engaged. That must sound strange and it is supposed to. Hang with me for a second. When I was madly in love, and before I proposed to my wife, I didn't think through the topic of money. I simply thought if it was important to me, it would be important to her. And besides, if she wasn't on the same page as I was, I would take care of it all and we'd be "good." I was wrong.

It Takes Teamwork

It takes both of you to be on the same page with your goals and how you think about money to truly be successful. One person can derail the entire process. The budgeting process described earlier needs to be carried out with both of you. However, before it can be implemented properly, you each need to have a say in how the future looks. It cannot be one person's idea with the expectation the other will get on board. That is where I went wrong. I needed to understand what made my wife feel secure (money-wise) and her perception of spending and saving. Additionally, I needed to tell her mine. If you think you want to save 50% of your take-home pay so you can be financially independent (and I hope you do), it takes sacrifice and dedication. It takes buy-in from your other. This is not going to work if you are running a dictatorship, because there will be a coup.

Before the Ring

Before I proposed, I should have taken the time to lay out where I stood financially. This can be embarrassing if you have debt (which I did). But, she was going to find out eventually, so why not do so ahead of time? If you are growing closer as a couple and it is leading toward engagement, you are close enough to expose yourself financially.

I am a fan of Dave Ramsey. If I could do it all again, I would have gone to one of his one-day seminars with my then girlfriend. Additionally, I would have worked my way through his Financial Peace series as a couple. That would serve as a forcing function to get you to talk through all aspects of money. If you are not a fan of his methods, use this book. It is such an easy read. You can read my mistakes, laugh at me with each other, and then ask, "So what do you think?" It will open a discussion and that is the point. Get to what you both will agree and get on the same plan ahead of time. Trust me, it is easier before you say "I do" than after. I read once that marriages end in divorce due to money issues more than any other reason. By taking the time to talk to each other about money ahead of time, you may end better than the statistics.

Forgetting Love (for one day)

What I mean by that is simply to put aside the romantic feelings for one day. Make a day out of it and tell your other, "I need to be honest with you about money and the future and I want you to be the same with me." Begin with your goals. Explain your vision, then work backward. Talk about how you want to become financially independent. Explain your reasoning. Then be honest and expose your own finances: how much you make, what you save, how much you owe. Most likely, this will be reciprocated. If not, it may be a warning sign. Don't push for it. Ask if they would be willing to share, too. If so, you will have upfront knowledge and enter an engagement without secrets. You will be a team and a dynamic team at that. It is too easy to stay blissfully ignorant and in love. Get serious for one day and learn more about one another. Interestingly, you will grow closer and your love will have depth.

If I had only known…

…about love, I would have loved my wife more by being honest with her about my personal finances before I proposed. I would have learned about her situation and we could have put together a game plan to be financially independent 15 years earlier than we did.

11

START AT COMMUNITY COLLEGE, FINISH AT UNIVERSITY

You may have heard the news: college is expensive! No surprise there, but you may not understand, fully, how to save a great deal of money on the cost of higher education. The secret? Local community college. Stay with me here. Don't get turned off by thinking no one will hire you based on a degree from the "trade college." That is ignorant thinking, and if you are not prepared to pay cash for a 4-year degree, you should pay close attention to this section.

Cost Savings

It all begins with saving money, right? I used real world numbers based off my hometown of Omaha, Nebraska. In Omaha, we have Metropolitan Community College that provides associate degrees and serves as a feeder to the University of Nebraska system. If you are inclined to pursue an accounting undergraduate degree at the university, you must take a total of 8 upper level accounting classes. Each one is a 3-hour course. 8 x 3 = 24 credit hours. But you must be well-rounded and that means you will need to take 15 credit hours in general education curriculum courses (English and writing, math, and public speaking). Additionally, you will need to complete 25 credit hours in distribution requirements (humanities and fine arts, social sciences, and natural and physical science). Lastly, you need 6 credit hours in diversity (U.S. and global). To sum it up: 46 credit hours before your upper level accounting courses. Therefore, 2/3 of your education is outside of the degree you are ultimately pursuing.

Let's put those math courses to work and see what would happen if you decided to take the 46 credit courses at the community college and transfer them to the university to complete the degree versus taking all courses at the university:

	Community College	University
$ per credit hour	$59[3]	$225[4]
$ of 46 credit hours	$2,714	$10,350

Difference: **$7,636!**

---

[3] https://www.mccneb.edu/Prospective-Students/Tuition-Financial-Assistance/Tuition.aspx
[4] http://admissions.unl.edu/cost.aspx

Or put another way, it costs 380% more to complete the basic classes at the university. There's more: lab fees, parking fees, student fees, fees for fees…. You get the point. Both places have them, but guess which is more expensive? Yep, you guessed right. I don't know about you, but I could use an extra $7,600 any day of the week. But there are additional reasons to choose the community college to begin.

Planning

When it comes to taking classes at the university, if you are a freshman or sophomore, you fall back of the line status when signing up for classes. It happened to me several times. The course I wanted was full or on the wrong day/time slot for my work schedule. I had to wait until next semester or choose another course (I usually chose another course. This by the way, is done on purpose to support the lessor classes no one would sign up, but I digress). At the community college, you are not fighting the large upper-class student population. It is easier to schedule classes, easier to find a parking spot, and here is a great reason: you can take classes while you are still in high school! This is a good time to transition to the best reason to take classes at the local community college and transfer over to the university.

Opportunity to Excel

You will have a chance to adjust to college, develop your study habits, and build confidence while distancing yourself from the potential pitfalls of freshman year beer bongs and craziness. I get it, it is fun to party, but really? You aren't reading this to be like everyone else; you are reading this to do better than everyone else. Some of the same instructors teaching at the university are also teaching at the community college. If you happen across them, you are, essentially getting the exact education at a discount. And let's play the game of educational standards for a moment. If the community college is easy and not "as good," then you will excel! You can be the proverbial big fish in the little pond (If you haven't read the book *David and Goliath* by Malcolm Gladwell, please do yourself the favor) and build great amounts of confidence. This confidence will transfer to the university along with all those sweet credits. Here is a major caveat: make sure you do the due diligence ensuring the community college is a feeder to the university.

The degree you receive from the university has its name on the diploma, not the community college name. Who cares where the basic courses were taken? Pass the upper level courses at the university and you get the degree!

If I had only known…

…about community colleges, I would have saved over $7,000 (worth $47,000 today!) and have the exact diploma hanging on my wall.

12
INDEXING IS BEST

There are myriad ways of investing your hard-earned savings, and I am going to be very clear up front: indexing is the way to go. I understand all the various techniques and I understand what it means to say to yourself, "Yes, indexing is best for the many, but I am one of the few and can do something different." You are wrong. You just are and I am not sorry to be the one to tell you. I understand you think you know better and I understand you have read, or listened to, others tell you active trading is better, but the numbers don't lie.

Ok, Numbers Do Lie

Numbers can be distorted or presented in a way to convince others the way they are presented is correct. This will happen with anyone trying to *sell* you an investment. (By the way, I just gave you a *huge* nugget. When someone is trying to get you to invest, they are selling you something. This can be ok, just understand what they are selling, and more importantly, how they are incentivized.) Personally, I can show you many different ways value investing is actually a great way to invest, but this book is short. This book is not going in-depth on every topic. This book is to give you the high level, 30,000-foot view of personal finance. You can do further research on this topic, or if you wish, reach out to me for a one-on-one discussion. The point is you should conduct due diligence and if you do, you will find that the time commitment for any other method of investing is a full-time job. Full time, not part time. I know you will have many people tell you how their hobby is investing and they are beating the market. When you hear this, please ask them to prove it. People have a way of lying to themselves and forgetting, or at least minimizing, the losses. No one cares about your money as much as you do. Be prudent.

Richest Man in the World Agrees

This is sort of misleading on purpose for a couple of reasons. First, I am referring to Warren Buffett, who is *not* the richest man in the world. However, if he hadn't given away a large portion of his wealth, he'd be the richest man. He is giving away great amounts of his wealth to the Bill and Melinda Gates Foundation, which is run by the actual richest man in the world: Bill Gates. The second reason this is misleading is because Warren Buffett isn't saying you should go the route of diversified indexing as I am, but he *has* directed the remaining investable money for his family to be invested in just <u>one</u> index fund. Here is what he wrote in his 2013 Annual Letter to Shareholders describing where the money he leaves his wife will be invested,

"My advice to the trustee could not be simpler: Put 10% of the cash in short-term government bonds and 90% in a very low-cost S&P 500 index fund (I suggest Vanguard's). I believe the trust's long-term results from this policy will be superior to those attained by most investors—whether pension funds, institutions or individuals—who employ high-fee managers."

Stop for a moment and think about what he wrote. This is the greatest investor of all time. He knows more than you, me, your full-service broker down the street or any on Wall Street. He has access to the best hedge funds in the world. And what exactly is that directive for his wife's investments? 10% into government bonds, **90%** into a Vanguard S&P 500 index fund. Why Vanguard? Because it is low cost. There are others that are low cost, too. Don't go into the weeds here; simply try to understand what he is saying: index with low cost mutual funds.

My Advice

You should get with a fee-based planner who isn't in it for the commissions. Ask them to help you determine your risk profile (or, you can figure it out on your own). Once you know the profile, invest in low-cost (look at the total cost of the mutual fund) index funds that will diversify you. Now, simply rebalance your portfolio each year. That is it. Congrats. You are well ahead of most people in the world. Best of all, you can sleep easy and you should be able to tell people what and how you are invested. It isn't rocket science when done properly.

If I had only known...

...about investing, I would have indexed long ago and stayed that way since I was 20 years old. Had I, there'd be an extra half million dollars in my investment account today. Ouch.

13
DON'T WASTE YOUR TALENT

This is the bonus chapter, and perhaps, the most important one. All of the previous chapters are things I learned about and implemented into my own life over the last several years. What I am about to share next was recently learned. It is fresh in my life and *very personal.*

Use Your Talents Now!

I love the game of football. I played it in high school and I've played pick-up games throughout life. I am pretty sure I got through high school simply because of the proverbial carrot dangling in front of me: playing football. I am not a big guy. I stand 5'7" and in high school I weighed 138 lbs. Suffice it to say colleges weren't kicking down my door throwing scholarships.

Over the years, I've watched several players in college and the pros take plays off. They didn't put enough effort behind their talent and I would say, "I'd give my left leg to play pro football. What a waste *this* guy is. He doesn't even know how lucky he is. I wish I had his talent; I would be unstoppable. I would give everything I had on *every* play." I went through most of my life like that, judging others, based on my perception of their effort level, but without knowing anything else about their life. How petty I am.

It has only occurred to me recently I have become that which I hate. Someone with immense talent wasting it. I have not put enough effort behind my talent. I have not played every play with gusto, with everything I have. The difference is my talent is not football (much to my chagrin); rather, my talents are helping others with personal finance, with investing, with debt elimination. I am good at public speaking. I can even write. Lastly, I am good at developing trust. I do this by simply being open and willing to share my failures. When I do, no one responds by kicking me while I am down. Instead, they respond with empathy, sharing their similar challenges. But having these talents and using them are two different things. It took until recently to learn this. No longer. I am now putting effort behind the talent.

In the Introduction, I shared the reasons I am writing this book: to spare someone else the mistakes I made. But there is more. I want to help others become wildly successful. So, please, take this last lesson from me and implement in your own life. Use your talents. Develop them. Put forth great effort. Don't take a play off, not one.

Life is too short to live with regret. I may wish I knew these things earlier and implemented them into my life, but I am not going to lament. Instead, I am going to share with others and ensure these types of mistakes don't continue. Additionally, I seek out people in my field who are 10 years or so older. I ask them, "What do you wish you knew at 42 that you didn't?" Or "What was your biggest challenge and how did you overcome it?" By asking these questions, can you see what I am doing? I am *knowing <u>NOW</u>* what they wish they knew *THEN!* Just like if the 22-year-old me was reading this book, I am getting my 52-year-old self to tell me what I should know. Why can't you do the same?

I think this is the most important thing to gather from this book: use your talents today and seek the wisdom of those who came before you. You have a great start with this book on the personal finance side of life. Now, look at other areas of your life and implement the same plan.

If I had only known…

…about using my talent, I would have honed my teaching, speaking, and writing skills earlier and used them to help others. Additionally, I would have sought out the wisdom of elders and begged and paid them to tell me what I didn't know and should.

CONCLUSION

I hope you have learned more than what you expected. I hope you have received *value* that far exceeds the small price you paid for this book. The concepts are condensed so you may begin immediately. You can conduct further research into each chapter and come up with your own game plan, but the point is to learn from my mistakes and move forward with prosperity.

What You Have Learned

You should now know that debt really is dangerous. It sets you back and handcuffs your future. Treat it with great caution and stay as far from it as possible. Understand the amount of money you save is way more important than how you invest it. Of course, you should invest in low-cost mutual funds and ensure you diversify properly based on your own risk profile. More importantly, the more you save as a percentage of your income, the quicker you will become financially independent. Once you do, you are powerful. No one can tell you what to do. You do what you want…like a winner!

You should take the time to really communicate early and often with your significant other. Ensure you are on the same page with each other when it comes to goals and how you see the future. The two of you will be dynamic if you are on the same page. You will be able to say no to your friends and family members if it is outside the budget. When you do, it will open up the opportunity for real conversation and you will be surprised to find you are encouraging them to do the same. It is a virtuous cycle.

You know a better way to attend college by starting at a local community college and transferring to the state school to earn your 4-year degree. The money you save will compound. That compound growth is vital to your wealth building. You MUST start early as time cannot be retrieved. Lastly, you know the less stuff you have, the simpler life can be, and that simplicity will lead to greater wealth.

Thank You

Thanks for reading. I hope to hear from you regarding your success. If you need further clarity on something, please feel free to reach out to me at Personal Finance Made Clear or Fourteen Forty

Financial Partners.

ABOUT THE AUTHOR

Mitchell C Hockenbury is an officer in the U.S. Army. Prior to commissioning as a Distinguished Graduate of the Army's Officer Candidate School, he worked in the investment industry helping families and small business owners plan for retirement. He has an MBA and undergraduate degrees in Finance and Banking.

The author continues to teach about money management and investing. He is married with a young daughter and resides in Kansas City, Missouri.